teach me about

Brothers and Sisters

Childrens Press
School and Library Edition
Published 1987

Managing Editor: Ellen Klarberg
Copy Editor: Kate Dickey
Contributing Writer: Kathleen McBride
Contributing Editors: Libby Byers, Maureen Dryden, Yona Flemming
Editorial Assistant: Sandy Passarino

Art Director: Laurie Westdahl
Design and Production: Abigail Johnston
Illustrator: Bartholomew
Inker: Caroline Rennard
Production Assistant: Lillian Cram
Composition: Curt Chelin

teach me about

Brothers and Sisters

By JOY BERRY

Illustrated by Bartholomew

CHILDRENS PRESS ®

CHICAGO

Some brothers and sisters are big.

Some brothers and sisters are little.

In some ways, all brothers and

sisters are the same.

Brothers and sisters want

their mommies and daddies to

love them.

If they think that

their mommies and daddies

do not love them,

brothers and sisters might feel sad.

7

Brothers and sisters want
their mommies and daddies
to pay attention to them.
When they think that their
mommies and daddies are
paying more attention
to a brother or sister,
they might feel jealous.

9

Brothers and sisters want
to be treated fairly.
When they think that another
person is getting more than
they are getting, brothers and
sisters might feel angry.

11

When brothers and sisters

think that another person

is being treated better,

they might feel left out.

Brothers and sisters do not want to be bothered while they are doing something important or interesting.

When another person bothers them, brothers and sisters might get angry.

15

Brothers and sisters do not want anyone to use their belongings without asking them if it is OK.

When another person uses their belongings without asking, brothers and sisters might get angry.

17

Brothers and sisters do not want their belongings to be broken or ruined.

When another person breaks their belongings, brothers and sisters might get angry.

Brothers and sisters do not want anyone to say mean things to them.

When another person says mean things to them, brothers and sisters might feel sad.

21

Brothers and sisters do not

want other children to tell

them what to do.

When other children are bossy,

brothers and sisters might

feel angry.

Brothers and sisters do not want anyone to hurt them. They do not want anyone to hit, kick, bite, or scratch them. They do not want anyone to pull their hair or push them. When someone hurts them, brothers and sisters might get very upset.

Your brothers and sisters

are special people.

Try to be good to them.

Do not bother them when they

are doing something

important or interesting.

27

Ask your brothers and sisters

if it is OK before you use

their belongings.

Use their belongings carefully

so you do not break them.

Try to be a good friend

to your brothers and sisters.

Do not say mean things

to them.

31

Try to remember that your

brothers and sisters do not

like to be bossed.

Do not tell them what to do.

Do not do anything to hurt

your brothers and sisters.

Do whatever you can to show

that you love them.